Insightful Thoughts for the Journey Through Life

BY ROBERT CHARLES AZAR

INTRODUCTION

This book is a collection of my original thoughts that I have written over the years that have helped me to deal with and grow through the challenges along the way in my Journey. They are insightful sayings, stimulating thoughts and encouraging reflections on Life, love and relationships that combine Eastern wisdom and Western philosophy. Some will warm your heart, others will encourage you to continue on your Journey with a new perspective. All are uplifting and are intended to empower us along the Journey Through Life.

While you may enjoy simply reading these sayings, I invite you to also make your experience of this book interactive. As you read each saying, feel free to jot down the thoughts and insights they bring out in you, making this a workbook for developing your own ideas and applications that you can go back and read time and again and benefit from. The "My Reflections" sections are included for this purpose.

Finally, I dedicate this book to my parents. To my father, Dr. Larry Azar, a professor of Western philosophy regarded by his colleagues and protégés as "the greatest mind in twentieth century American philosophy", my thanks for cultivating in me a strong philosophical view of Life and the world. To my mother, my thanks for demonstrating what Life and love are all about through her constant caring and sacrifice.

Robert C. Azar
Cary, North Carolina
U.S.A.

Life is short... But it sure seems to take the long way in getting there.

~ *My Reflections* ~

Our inner Beauty
illuminates our life.

~ *My Reflections* ~

*Some people drive through Life
with their headlights on.
Others drive through Life with
only their parking lights on.
Still others don't even realize
that they're supposed to
turn their lights on...
Let's go through Life with
our high beams on!*

~ *My Reflections* ~

Let's always seek the big picture with patience and understanding, realizing that even in a masterpiece painting not every brushstroke is perfect.

~ My Reflections ~

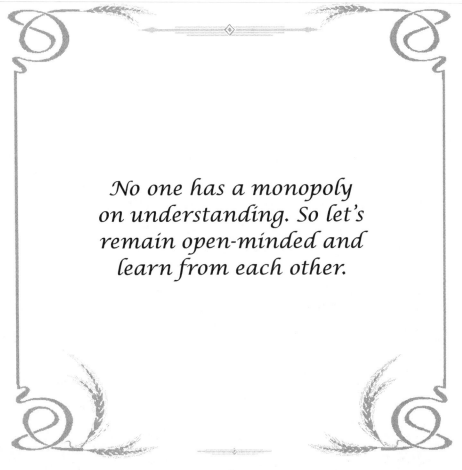

*No one has a monopoly
on understanding. So let's
remain open-minded and
learn from each other.*

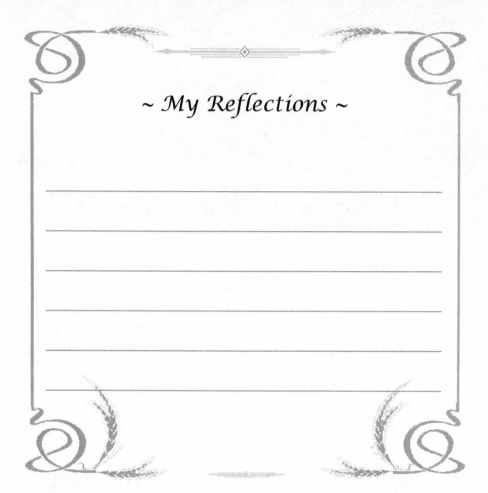

~ *My Reflections* ~

May I have the wisdom
and humility to allow my
life to unfold in the way
that is best for me.

~ *My Reflections* ~

It is so very important that we be our own best friend in Life.

~ My Reflections ~

Love is the closest thing to Heaven.

~ *My Reflections* ~

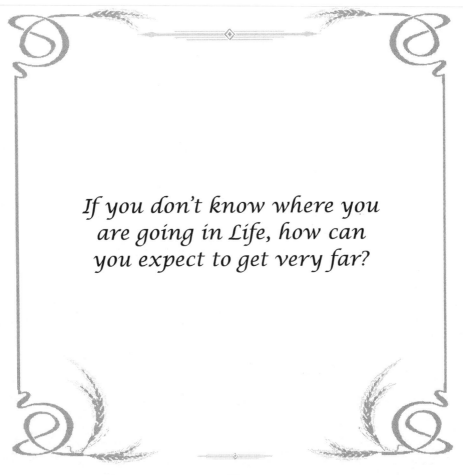

If you don't know where you are going in Life, how can you expect to get very far?

~ My Reflections ~

The future is created today, not tomorrow.

~ My Reflections ~

When we have our nose up against a tree, we can't see the forest. Let's step back and benefit from a panoramic and holistic view of what Life brings our way.

~ *My Reflections* ~

When we grow, we live.
When we do not grow,
we simply exist.

~ My Reflections ~

Our character, beliefs, values, outlooks, sensibilities, and the way we interact with and impact others determine who we are as individuals. These are what define our inner Beauty. It is our inner Beauty that prompts us to make the Life decisions that we do.

~ My Reflections ~

*We are on this earth and we
have the experiences we do in
Life in order to blossom into
our full-growth potential as
the unique individual each of
us is. Celebrate the Journey!*

~ *My Reflections* ~

There is no need to compare your self to others. We are not in competition with other people. We are only in competition with ourselves – that is, to develop from where we are today to reaching our full-growth potential. Being the best we can possibly be – that is our greatest challenge and measure of who we should be.

~ *My Reflections* ~

*The curve balls that Life
so often throws at us are
designed to shake us up so
that we may grow to the next
stage in our development.*

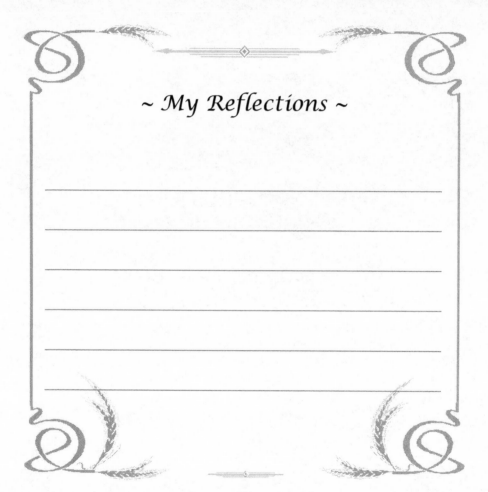

~ My Reflections ~

Our ultimate challenge and goal is to be able to love as selflessly as God Himself loves.

~ *My Reflections* ~

What I believe in:

· *I believe in the Supreme Being. I strive to recognize, acknowledge and respect the Divine presence in all things.*

· *I believe that there are definite spiritual and ethical principles that provide order and structure to the Universe. I seek to live in accordance with these Universal laws.*

~ My Reflections ~

*It is not necessary for me to
get angry or frustrated by
what others do. The fact that
their actions upset me means
that those actions go against
my beliefs and values. If those
actions were of a higher order
I would be inspired by them,
not feel bothered by them. I can
only be angered by actions of
a lower order. So let's always
aim high and not allow actions
of a lower order to upset us.*

~ *My Reflections* ~

My life belongs not just to me, but also to God who gave it to me. In light of this, may what I return – through the person I evolve into, the way I live my life and how I give back – reflect this.

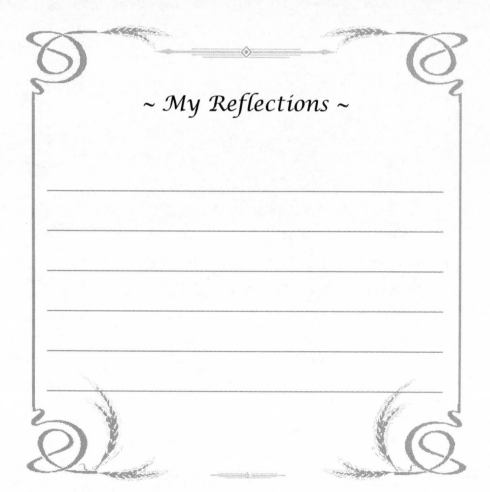

~ My Reflections ~

*It is in human fellowship
that some of Life's greatest
pleasures are found.*

~ My Reflections ~

We are all endowed with profound inner peace. Let's take the time to connect with it and benefit from it.

~ *My Reflections* ~

Time waits for no one.

~ *My Reflections* ~

It is only after we let go of the things that seem to be important that we can appreciate those things that actually are.

~ My Reflections ~

Uncertainty and crisis in our lives can be a catalyst for our growth and improvement. Instead of allowing uncertainty and hardship to get the better of us, let's rise to the occasion with positive expectation.

~ My Reflections ~

We tend to see ourselves
and the world around us
through our own eyes.
When we do, we greatly shortchange ourselves of who we are
and what we can become.
That is because our own
viewpoint sees us where we
are in the present moment
and has little idea as to what
our future potential and
destination in Life are.

~ *My Reflections* ~

*Let's be humble enough to allow
the Universe to work in our life.*

~ *My Reflections* ~

Life and relationships are not a collection of snapshots taken along the way. Instead they are videos that are constantly turned on and recording. So let's make the best of each moment!

~ My Reflections ~

*Life is a sacred trust from God,
who endows each of us richly.
How wisely we develop and use
our ability determines how much
interest our life will return to
God. And also determines how
much fulfillment we will attain.*

~ *My Reflections* ~

*Love is the greatest gift we
can give to each other!*

~ My Reflections ~

I view my life as standing on the shoulders of those who have come before me, whether they be my parents, teachers, sages, historical figures. I ask how can I contribute to elevating the human pyramid? This is our life-long aim.

~ *My Reflections* ~

We often look at other people, situations and even Life itself with ourselves at the center. We think what can I gain from that person? How will that situation benefit me? And so on... How greatly we shortchange ourselves. Shortchange our encounters with others. Shortchange our very experience of Life itself. It's when we first think how can I contribute to the greater good that the best in each of us is elevated.

~ *My Reflections* ~

*Our self-mind (ego) seeks to fulfill
the needs only of one's self. In
contrast, the Universal mind
within us seeks to fulfill the needs
of the entire Universe. Since
all of our needs are included
within the Universe, doesn't it
make sense to seek the guidance
and joy of the Universal
mind within each of us?*

~ My Reflections ~

Our self-mind (ego) can never be satisfied because it is in constant pursuit of endless wants. In contrast, our Universal mind is designed to naturally find peace and equilibrium. All we have to do is tune into it.

~ *My Reflections* ~

*Life is not a rush toward a
certain goal or endpoint,
but is a Journey that
we're meant to enjoy and
appreciate along the way.*

~ My Reflections ~

When we look at a calm lake, we can see not only the bottom of the lake but also the sky and the other side of the lake reflected on the water's surface. However, when the water becomes rough, we cannot see any of them. Instead we only see the choppy water on the surface. It is the same lake, but what we can see and how clearly we can see it is totally different depending on the calmness of the water. This is true in our lives as well. When things are calm, we tend to see things clearly. But when something upsets our lives, we often are no longer able to see things clearly. We're the same individuals, but our ability to understand is diminished. Ah, the importance of maintaining our Inner Calm in the face of Life's storms.

~ *My Reflections* ~

When confronting Life's storms, seek the eye of the storm – our Inner Calm.

~ *My Reflections* ~

As a child, I was always
intrigued by the kaleidoscope.
As an adult, I try to
apply the dynamic of the
kaleidoscope to Life.
Just as the slightest turn of
the kaleidoscope completely
changed what I would see, the
slightest change in my attitude
and outlook can totally change
the realities of my life.

~ *My Reflections* ~

Life is too short to allow our hurt from the past to prevent us from enjoying a full and complete life in the present and future. Let's deal with our issues so we may experience a fulfilled life.

~ My Reflections ~

What goes around comes around – with interest!

~ *My Reflections* ~

Since Life is a process of self-growth, approach all things as steps along the way.

~ My Reflections ~

A heavy object may be difficult to pick up. That same heavy object in water, however, becomes so much easier to lift and move around. That is what it means to be in one's element. Everything comes more easily, more effortlessly, and so naturally. Fortunate are those who can find and live in their element.

~ My Reflections ~

*I believe that some of
Life's greatest pleasures
are its simplest ones.*

~ My Reflections ~

The most profound Truths in Life are the simplest.

~ My Reflections ~

Our life is God's gift to us. So let's strive to make our impact on others be God's gift to them.

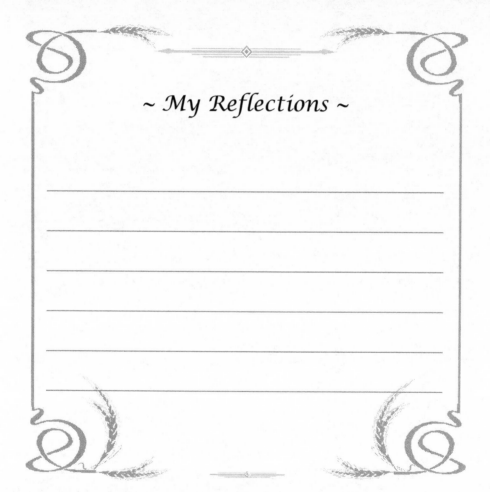

~ *My Reflections* ~

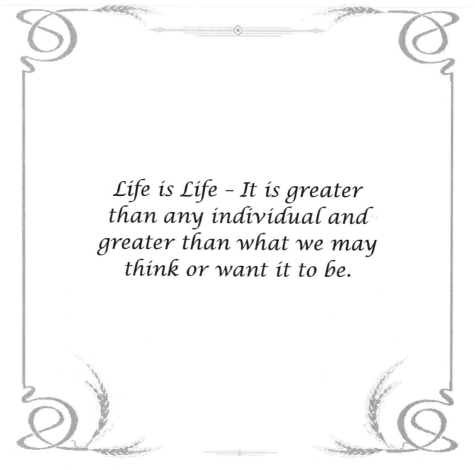

*Life is Life – It is greater
than any individual and
greater than what we may
think or want it to be.*

~ *My Reflections* ~

Life has a life of its own – No matter how we may want it to be, it will unfold as it will.

~ My Reflections ~

*One's true direction in Life
can only be known when
we are in harmony with the
Universe's intention for us.*

~ My Reflections ~

*Seek to do Good for the Universe
and other people, and the
Goodness of the Universe and
other people can come to you.*

~ My Reflections ~

The way of the Universe is not "give and take". It's give, and then receive.

~ My Reflections ~

Love is giving of oneself to fulfill the needs of another.

~ My Reflections ~

*An integral part of Leadership
is creating constructive change
even when that change is
neither welcome nor popular –
or even seemingly impossible.*

~ My Reflections ~

The ultimate measure or success of a life is not how a resume or bank statement reads. Rather how much we have loved and helped others.

~ My Reflections ~

The secret to inner peace is transcending one's own ego – rising above the clatter and clutter in our minds. We do that by letting go and focusing on the Universal mind within.

~ My Reflections ~

*Like the lotus flower whose roots
start out in the muddy bottom
of the pond and yet ends up
blooming beautifully on the
water's surface, we also need
to rise above the uncertainties
that sometimes come our
way and cultivate our Inner
Beauty so that it may blossom
and help beautify the world.*

~ *My Reflections* ~

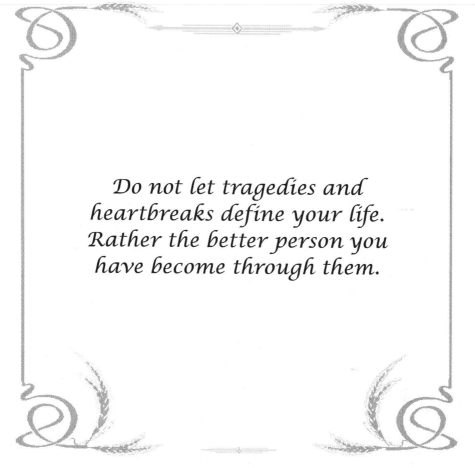

Do not let tragedies and heartbreaks define your life. Rather the better person you have become through them.

~ My Reflections ~

Faith is our trust and hope in God.

~ *My Reflections* ~

*Nothing positive comes
out of negativity.*

~ My Reflections ~

Negativity is like quicksand – the more we wallow in it, the deeper we sink into it. And the harder it is to get out... So let's avoid it to begin with and steer our lives positively.

~ My Reflections ~

The only constant in Life is change.

~ My Reflections ~

We often tend to fear change. However, fear of change comes from not knowing what will result from it. Why not at least wait and see what the new circumstances will be first before we allow ourselves to get bent out of shape by fear of change.

~ *My Reflections* ~

*Nothing is so beautiful as
the act of giving of oneself
for the sake of another.*

~ My Reflections ~

Be genuine in all that you do.
Other people are not dumb
and can intuitively sense
where you are coming from.

~ *My Reflections* ~

It's all so simple... once you know it.

~ *My Reflections* ~

Life is meant to be shared. We are not here just for ourselves but for those the Universe brings into our lives as well.

~ My Reflections ~

While we may be content, going through Life all by our self is like experiencing it in black and white. When we go through Life sharing it with loved ones we experience it in Living Color.

~ *My Reflections* ~

When we fly through Life solo, we experience it two dimensionally. Sharing Life with those we love enables us to experience it three dimensionally.

~ My Reflections ~

When it comes to Love,
the more the merrier.

~ My Reflections ~

I believe that when God creates us, He makes us all at the 100% level. So we are all equal. How that 100% manifests itself in us is what gives us our unique personalities and abilities.

~ *My Reflections* ~

I believe we are all but one piece in God's Grand Mosaic of humanity. Even though we may be endowed with different abilities, we are all equal in value and importance. For any mosaic would be incomplete missing even just one piece – no matter how small or seemingly unimportant.

~ My Reflections ~

We are all VIPs!

~ *My Reflections* ~

Negative thoughts play the loudest in our minds. So let's take a few moments in our day to quiet our mind and focus on positive, validating and healing thoughts... This is the essence of meditation and stress management.

~ *My Reflections* ~

How wonderful is the grand symphony of my thoughts. And I thought Grand Central Station in New York City at rush hour was bustling!

~ My Reflections ~

In Life, do what you can
when you can for you
never know when you will
no longer be able to.

~ *My Reflections* ~

I want my relationships
with others to be based
upon mutual respect.
My interactions with others will
be positive and constructive.
They will enrich the
lives of others.
Each interaction in each
relationship will take me
one step closer to my
full-growth potential.
And help others to do the same.

~ My Reflections ~

Relationships are built on the common ground you share. So the more you have in common, the stronger the foundation for your relationship.

~ *My Reflections* ~

It is easy to find ways to look down on and criticize others. It takes a lot more character and courage to find ways to lift each other up.

~ My Reflections ~

Don't worry whether you are too tall or short. Instead we all should develop meaningful reasons why others will want to look up to us.

~ My Reflections ~

There's a path for everyone in Life. The key is finding it... So why don't we strive to help each other do just that! Let's be encouraging and affirming with each other.

~ My Reflections ~

No one enjoys becoming disillusioned. However, I've come to realize that it can help us get rid of the illusions we sometimes hold onto. Sometimes we read into a person or situation more than is really there – in other words, we carry an illusion about them...

~ My Reflections ~

If we want to make better choices in Life, then we need to improve the outlooks, beliefs and values that they are based on. This is a fundamental part of our inner growth.

~ *My Reflections* ~

When something comes across
your Path that you fear, think
of something you fear more.

~ My Reflections ~

When looking within, we sometimes find areas we don't care for – places we would prefer not to go to. But often it is not necessary to enter all the way into a totally dark room in order to understand what is inside. All we have to do is open the door a crack, slip our finger in and turn on the lights. The darkness disappears immediately... Let's find the courage to turn on the lights!

~ My Reflections ~

When we reach a certain level in life it's time to give back. Let's help others along their Journey by sharing the experiences and insights we have been fortunate to gain along the way.

~ My Reflections ~

In our daily lives, we often run on auto pilot as we deal with the numerous demands on our time, attention and emotional energy. When we get out of our normal environment and routine we are no longer occupied by the "usual things", and are much more receptive to new possibilities and ways of looking at things that can enhance our lives... It is so important to step outside of the daily hustle and bustle and reflect.

~ My Reflections ~

When you try something new and it does not work out, don't beat yourself up over it. That just means it is not for you... Let's appreciate those opportunities to better understand ourselves.

~ My Reflections ~

We can only do our best – our 100%.
There is no 110%. All we can do
is our best... So let's strive to do our
very best in all things and be
content with that, remembering
that so much in Life is simply
beyond our control.

~ My Reflections ~

No matter what may come our way in Life, let's try to land on our feet a better, deeper, more compassionate individual. This is what our Journey is all about.

~ My Reflections ~

*Let's not defeat ourselves!
No matter how painful our
experiences in Life, whether we
give up our hopes and ideals
or not is entirely up to us. It's
our choice, and our choice
alone... Let's be strong and
hold onto our better selves.*

~ My Reflections ~

AUTHOR BIOGRAPHY

Robert Charles Azar is a distinguished intercultural expert who has dedicated his life to mastering and bridging the gap between Eastern and Western cultures. A citizen of the United States, he spent seven years living in the Far East and thirty-five years working in US-Asian business and cultural mediation, where he helped both sides navigate differences in culture, values, practices, and perspectives.

Azar holds a BA in international relations and East Asian studies from New York University, an MA in East Asian political, economic, and cultural affairs from Columbia University, and he studied global management at Harvard University. He has taught extensively on these subjects; has been interviewed as an expert on these topics by major media in America and Japan such as CNN, BusinessWeek, and the New York Times; and has published articles in numerous American and Japanese journals. He also paints Japanese calligraphy and is fluent in reading, writing and speaking Japanese.

Through his education and experiences, Azar has developed fresh and unique insights and well-tuned wisdoms, which are collected in his debut title, *Insightful Thoughts for the Journey through Life.*

Made in the USA
Charleston, SC
09 April 2016